Travel With Kids

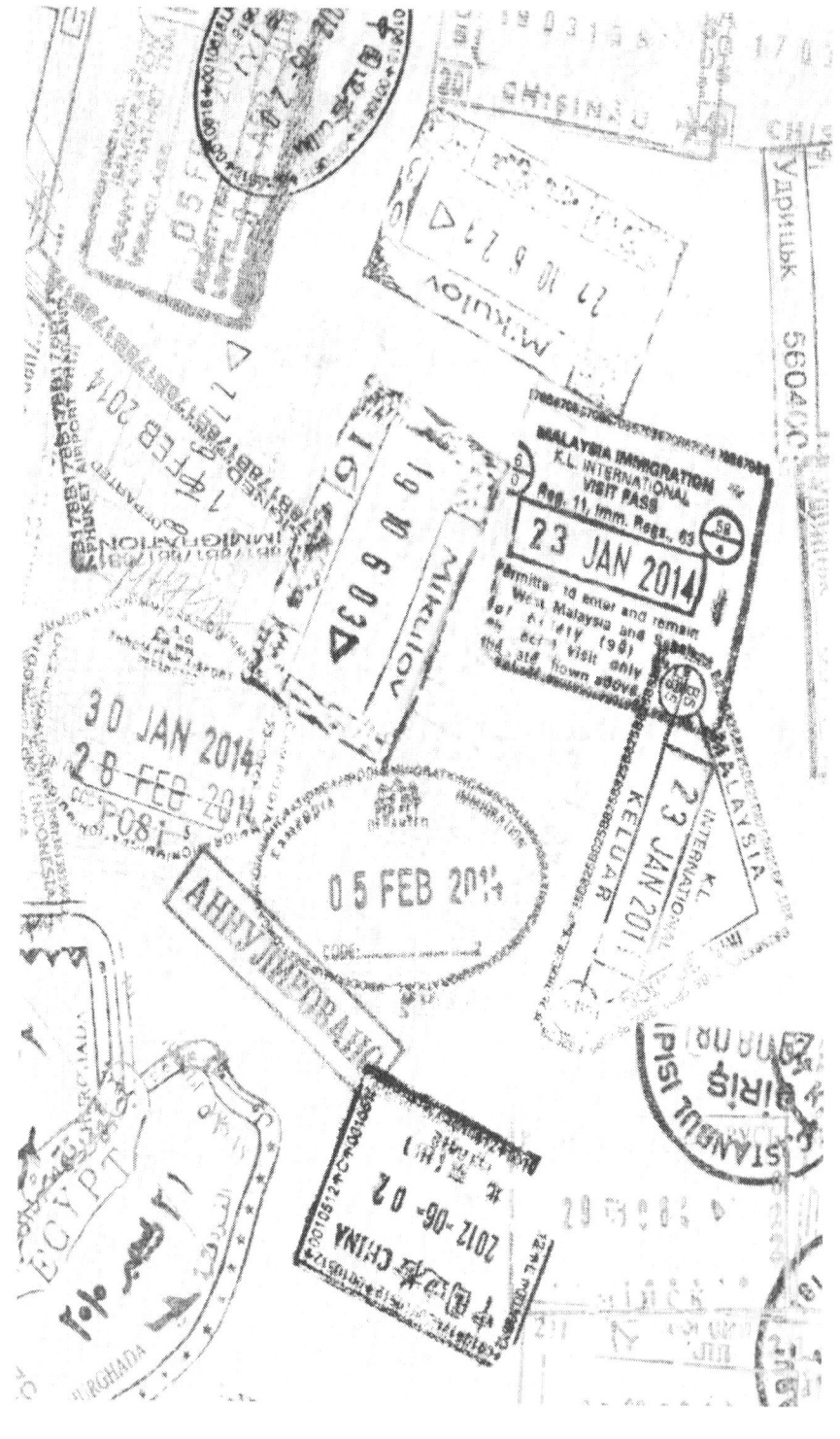

Travel With Kids

Edward Cox

Nomadic Dragon Books

Honolulu

NOMADIC DRAGON BOOKS

Published in the United States of America
by Nomadic Dragon Books, P.O. Box 30800 PMB 194
Honolulu, HI 96820-0800
www.NomadicDragon.com

Copyright © 2017 by Nomadic Dragon Books

Author photo © 2014 by Hannah Brown, Roots and Leaves Photography. Used with permission.

All rights reserved. No part of this publication may be reproduced or transmitted in any form or by any means, electronic or mechanical, including photocopy, or any information storage or retrieval system, without permission in writing from the publisher.

Library of Congress Control Number: 2017903508

ISBN: 978-0-9971326-2-5

To my parents
who opened my eyes to the world
around me

And

To Ellyn
my constant companion

Contents

Foreword	1
Chapter 1 – The Key to Successful Travel	5
Chapter 2 – All About Budgeting	9
Chapter 3 – The How – Trip Selection	19
Chapter 4 – The Where – Site Selection	27
Chapter 5 – Preparation is King	33
Chapter 6 – Expectation Management	45
Chapter 7 – And We're Off!	51
Chapter 8 – Culture Shock	59
Chapter 9 – Surviving Re-entry	63
Chapter 10 – Travel with Infants	67
Chapter 11 – Travel with Teenagers	71
Chapter 12 – Lifelong Travel	75
Chapter 13 – Travel Resources	81
Acknowledgements	87
Index	88

Foreword

    I'm sure my fascination with travel is partly due to living overseas as a child. I spent several years as a young child and two years of high school in Europe. I liked it so much that I moved back to Europe shortly after graduating from college. I visited new cities on long weekends like Barcelona and Munich. I got married and we traveled as a couple to Dublin, Berlin, and Rome. Then we found out that my wife was pregnant.

    I had the idea for this book the first time someone told us that we'd have to stop traveling now that we had kids. Every time we planned a trip and had to endure the doubts and questions of friends and family, it strengthened my resolution to write it. From time to time while working on the manuscript, I've seen this "conventional wisdom" crop up in the media as well. I read an editorial on the subject. I overheard a discussion about it at a coffee shop. These incidents renewed my enthusiasm for this project every time my motivation to continue writing lagged. Maybe I'm just contrarian by nature. Or maybe it's because I truly believe that travel is one of the best gifts that you can give your kids.

We took our first overseas trip with our kids when the youngest one was less than a year old. We spent eight hours on a plane across the Pacific. We celebrated his first birthday in Japan. We negotiated the Tokyo subway system with a stroller. We spent one morning walking around Kyoto at 6 a.m. waiting for restaurant to open, because my kids were so noisy that we got kicked out of our ryokan. And I would do it all over again. In the ten years since then, we've gone to over a dozen more countries and we aren't stopping.

I'd be lying if I said we loved every minute of it. But we discovered, or rather rediscovered, that it was possible and pleasant to travel. Even with kids. Is it cheap? Well, that depends on a lot of factors that I'll discuss later. It can be more difficult than traveling on your own. It can be frustrating and time-consuming at times. It doesn't always show an immediate payback on the time and money you spent doing it. I might add that the same can be said of parenting as a whole. It is still worth it.

Most, if not all, of the things that we want our children to know about the world, they learned through travel. They've learned that not everyone in the world has the same blessings that they have. That over half the world struggles to make a living on less than their allowance. I hope that this had made them more grateful for what they have. More willing to give to others. Most days it seems that it has. They've learned that not everyone has the same beliefs that they do, but that they hold those beliefs just as dearly. This has caused them to examine their own beliefs and that has made them stronger. It has also helped them to be more tolerant. They've seen wonders both natural and man-made. Most of all, they've learned that people everywhere are the same. They have the same innate needs and desires. They have dreams.

Travel, especially international travel, is out of reach for many people. But they are likely not reading this book. You are. Maybe you're debating whether it would be worth all the hassle. Maybe you've dreamed of doing this but you aren't sure how to get started. You're wondering how much it will cost, where to go, and what to see when you get there. This book was written to help you do just that.

This book is short. On purpose. I don't want you to curl up with another 400-page tome and think about how you might travel someday. I want you to read it quickly and get on the road.

Maybe you've taken a trip that turned out to be a disaster and you're wondering why anyone would ever do that again. This book was written to help you have a better trip next time.

I'm here to tell you that it's worth it to try. It's worth it to try again. Take the plunge. Open that door (or re-open it) and see what happens. There's a whole world out there waiting to be seen.

Go see the world. Take the kids.

Chapter 1
The Key to Successful Travel

In a 2014 survey, 42% of Americans did not take a single vacation day that year. In 2005, Gallup reported that only 27% of teenagers had ever left the country. It is estimated that less than half of all Americans even have a current passport.

America has a reputation for insularity when it comes to travel. There are a lot of reasons for that. Many Americans only get one to two weeks of vacation every year. International travel almost always involves travel by air, which can get expensive. America is immense, and many Americans find plenty to see within the country's borders without feeling the need to journey overseas.

All of these seem like valid reasons until you realize that this insularity is not unique to Americans. A recent survey of the British found that 1 in 5 has never left the United Kingdom. Bear in mind that it's only an hour and a half by boat from Dover to Calais, France. There are over three dozen departures daily. It's only two hours from London to Paris by bullet train.

Key to Successful Travel

There are many obstacles to travel. Lack of money or time. Safety concerns. Objections by grandparents or a spouse. Rather than look at the obstacles, however, I've chosen to look at the keys to making travel with kids successful, affordable, and enjoyable. Here are my five keys to successful travel with kids. Each gets a chapter of its own. I've also included chapters about travel with two very distinct groups of kids, infants and teenagers.

- Budgeting
- Trip selection
- Site selection
- Preparation
- Expectation Management

Budgeting

In 2015, New York Times columnist David Brooks wrote a piece titled "My $120,000 Vacation." He described a 24-day world tour arranged by the Four Seasons company using a private jet and luxury hotels. If you have that kind of budget for family travel, congratulations. If not, spend a little time thinking about how much you want to spend on your trip. Do this step first because it sets up the framework for the rest of the planning. This chapter also covers how to save for travel and how to use airline miles and hotel points to offset your costs.

Trip Selection

This is the "how" of your travel. Are you going to make it a long-weekend getaway? A family excursion in conjunction with business travel? How you decide to travel will impact where you decide to travel.

Site Selection

Site selection deals with the "where" of your trip. This means more than just the country that you're going to, however. Spend some time thinking about the features that you want in a destination – urban vs. rural, mountains vs. beaches, tropical vs. temperate.

Preparation

Preparation is king. How you prepare for your trip directly contributes to the success or failure of the trip. Preparation includes arranging passports and visas, immunizations, language training, and lots more.

Expectation Management

Managing expectations means remembering that the kids you bring with you are the same kids that you have at home. If they get tired and cranky at home, they will get tired and cranky in Rome. If they show little interest in history, don't think a museum tour is going to change that. This doesn't mean you shouldn't travel. Rather, it means that you should plan your trip with your kids in mind. They won't get everything that you want them to. And that's okay. They will get something out of it. I promise.

Chapter 2
All About Budgeting

You can afford it. Most Americans with a middle-class income could comfortably spend 2-3 weeks in any location in the world for vacation. It just takes planning and prioritizing.

Your budget is going to depend on the size of your family, your destination, and the duration of your trip. Traveling during off-season or outside of the major school holidays is cheaper. Travel in developing countries will be cheaper. Slower travel is also cheaper than fast travel. As an example, here are three ways to get from Singapore to Kuala Lumpur, Malaysia, a distance of 220 miles.

    Fly - 1 hour, $92
    Bus – 6 hours, $16
    Train – 8 hours, $22

Flying only takes an hour but costs 4-5 times more. If you have time to travel slower, you will save money. Your four biggest expenses will be transportation, lodging, food, and attractions. Below are recommendations on how to make family travel more affordable in each of those areas.

Save Money on Airfare

You can use frequent flier miles to get tickets if you have them. Outside of that, you're probably buying tickets for this trip.

One theory holds that plane tickets are cheaper if you buy them on a Tuesday. Another theory holds that the best time to purchase is two months before you fly. Others will say book tickets six months before you fly. Travel in the off-season. Fly mid-week.

You could drive yourself crazy trying to game this. Don't. Go to a good website like Skyscanner or ITA Matrix. Find tickets. Buy them. Move on.

If you're traveling by train in Europe, Japan, or Korea, look into rail passes. These passes allow you to travel as much as you want for a given number of days. The Eurail pass has several options based on the number of countries you plan to visit and how many days you plan to travel. Do your research – the Japanese rail pass has to be purchased before you arrive in Japan.

Save Money on Lodging

Children take up more space as they grow older. At some point, that means you need to get two or more hotel rooms instead of one. Getting connecting rooms will allow you to keep an eye on the kids but it can get expensive. It's also not always feasible outside the U.S.

A cheaper solution is to rent a house or apartment. It's even cheaper if you travel with another family and pool your resources.

Another option is to stay at a hostel. Most people think of hostels as cheap accommodations for college kids backpacking through Europe. Many hostels offer budget lodging for families as well and are clean and safe.

If you want to stay at a hotel, look beyond the main U.S. brands that you are familiar with. They are the names that you recognize, but there are lots of other reputable hotel chains outside the U.S.

If you are going to stay at hotels, especially U.S. brands, consider using hotel points. There's an entire subculture in the travel world devoted to maximizing and using hotel points. A good resource to start researching this is the Extra Pack of Peanuts website by Travis Sherry.

Sign-up bonuses for credit cards linked to hotel chains can pay for 2-3 nights depending on location and time of year. Use this to off-set costs. For example, book 3 nights with points and pay for 3 nights with cash.

Save Money on Meals

If breakfast is included in your hotel rate, take full advantage of that. If it isn't, skip the hotel breakfast. It's convenient and expansive. It's also probably one of the most expensive ways to get breakfast. Instead, go get breakfast on the road. Or plan ahead and get some food the night before to eat in your room.

Stop at a local grocery store and pick up materials for a picnic lunch. Now you're only eating out for dinner, which is much more economical than eating out three meals a day.

If you have access to a kitchen, go to the local grocery store and get groceries to cook at home.

Save Money on Attractions

If you're going to hit the tourist highlights of a city, look into discount passes. These passes allow you free or discount admission to the main sights of a city with the purchase of a prepaid pass. European cities with passes like this include London, Paris, Barcelona, Berlin, Dublin and Vienna. Cities in Asia with discount passes include Taipei, Tokyo, Hong Kong, Singapore, and Colombo. The initial price of these passes is steep, but they prove worth it if you are going to hit multiple sites during your visit. I suggest doing the math to determine when you've hit the break-even point to recoup the purchase price.

If You Have Debt, Don't Travel

This is a personal rule that I believe in strongly. Travel can be life-changing but it shouldn't create debt or keep you from getting rid of debt. Many people have a home mortgage. In this case, I don't count that as debt. If you have credit card debt, however, I strongly recommend paying it off before planning any international travel.

Sample budgets

I hesitate to list sample budgets for two reasons. First, everyone's budget will depend on size of family, hometown, and interests. Second, prices change by the minutes for airfare and almost as frequently for hotels. Two identical families traveling to and from the same locations could pay vastly different prices based on how far in advance they make their bookings and personal preferences.

With those caveats in place, here are a few sample budgets. Each one assumes that you already have passports. Use these as a rough guide.

Miami to Caribbean
Family of four, 2 young children (under 6)
1 week

Ports of call
- Netherlands Antilles
- San Juan, Puerto Rico
- Bahamas
- 3 nights at sea

Cruise – 7 night Caribbean cruise One stateroom	$1,280
Shore activities	$400
Tips	$110
Total	$1,790

Chicago to Montreal
Family of three, 1 teenager
Long weekend

Airfare	$1,133
Hotel	$738
4-star hotel	
2 connecting rooms	
3 nights @ $123 / night / room	
includes breakfast	
Food	$135
$45 / day	
City Pass	$252
$84 / per person	
good for 48 hours	
includes use of public transport	
Souvenirs	$100
Total	$2,358

Save $350 by staying at a hostel.
Save $368 by using points for one plane ticket

All About Budgeting

Los Angeles to Seoul
Family of four, 1 teenager
9 nights, Christmas break

Airfare	$7,238
Traditional home, 9 nights	$990
Historic district	
2 connecting rooms	
includes breakfast	
Food	$550
$55 / day	
City Pass	$120
$30 / per person	
good for 3 days	
public transport	
DMZ tour	$312
Souvenirs and misc	$350
Total	$9,560

Save $3619 by using points for two plane tickets

Houston to Antigua, Guatemala
Family of four
2 weeks

Airfare	$1,278
House rental	$588
Airbnb	
Entire house with kitchen	
2 weeks @ $42 / night	
Food	$150
Transport	$100
Includes taxis to/from airport	
Souvenirs	$100
Total	$2,216

Atlanta to Rome
Family of three
8 days

Airfare	$3,290

House rental
    Airbnb
    Entire home with kitchen
    7 nights @ $110 / night
	$770

Food $45 / day	$360

City Pass
    $113 / per person
    good for 72 hours
    includes Vatican and Rome
    includes use of public transport
	$339

Souvenirs	$200
Total	$4,959

New York to London
Single parent, 2 teenagers
Long weekend (2 nights)

Airfare	$1,738
Overnight flight to London	
Home Monday afternoon	
Hotel	$592
3-star hotel	
2 connecting rooms	
2 nights @ $148/ night / room	
includes breakfast	
Food	$195
$65 / day	
City Pass	$309
$103 / per person	
good for 48 hours	
$15 public transport credit	
Souvenirs	$200
Total	$3,034

Chapter 3
The How - Trip Selection

Trip Selection

There are as many ways to travel internationally as there are families. How you travel will depend on your time, your family, your budget and your interests. If you've never taken your kids overseas, I recommend starting with a weekend trip or a cruise. Think of these as "shake-outs," trips to help you work out the kinks in your systems before you take off on a world tour.

I've categorized trips in a few different ways below to get you thinking.
- Weekender
- Cruise
- Business Plus
- Visit friends

- Themed trip
- Grand Vacation
- Round the World voyage

Weekender

When I was in college, a friend of mine discovered that it was cheaper for him to fly to Paris, France for a three-day weekend than it was to fly home to Mississippi. Naturally, he asked around to see if anyone else wanted to join him. Naturally, I said yes, along with a few dozen others. After a few months of planning, we were standing atop the Eiffel Tower over Presidents' Day weekend. I've been back to Paris three times since, but I still remember something special about that first weekend.

A weekend trip can be a quick way to experience another culture cheaply, especially if you take advantage of airline ticket sales in the off-season. The downside is that two or three days doesn't give you very much time. You'll want to focus on hitting the highlights of your destination. This is not hard, since many travel books have sample itineraries based on your length of stay. You'll probably still be recovering from jet lag when you get home, so the first day or two back at work will be rough. I will say, however, that "flew to Paris" is still one of my favorite answers to the question, "what did you do this weekend?"

Time is one of the greatest limiting factors on a weekend trip. If you live on the East coast, aim for Quebec, Canada or a major European city. Catching a Friday evening flight should put you on the ground Saturday morning (the time zones work in your favor here). You'll fly back early Monday morning and arrive late on Monday evening, just in time to put the kids to bed. Everyone will be tired the next day. It generally takes one day to recover for every hour of time zone shift. After about a week things will be back to normal.

This kind of trip is also feasible from the Midwest, since there are dozens of international flights departing from major hubs like Chicago. The farther west you live, however, the more likely it is that you'll want to aim for Canada, Mexico, or the Caribbean. Flight times to Asia make a weekend trip impractical. Europe is only within reach if you spend the whole day Friday traveling.

Cruise

A cruise is one of the easiest ways to travel overseas. The cruise ship functions as a floating hotel with restaurants and shops included. The popular cruise lines all have staff dedicated to programs for kids, allowing for some time alone as a couple. You only have to unpack once.

Most of the cruise itineraries familiar to Americans stay in the Caribbean. In a one-week cruise, you'll visit 4-5 countries and spend one day at each port. You won't see much of the country in a day. In fact, critics would argue that the experience you'll get is far from authentic. Shopping for souvenirs just off the ship in Nassau or Basseterre is not the same experience as venturing to the Out Islands or Charlestown. Whether you agree or not depends on your objectives for the trip. If you're looking for an in-depth exploration of one culture complete with language immersion, then a Caribbean cruise is not the right option. If you're looking for an easy way to get out of the country and start traveling, it might just be the way to go. For a longer trip that's farther afield, consider a transatlantic cruise or a Mediterranean cruise. A transatlantic cruise won't have very many port calls, if any.

A repositioning cruise occurs when cruise lines move ships from one part of the world to another. A ship that sails in the Caribbean in the winter, for example, might cross through the Panama Canal and sail up to west coast of the U.S. in the spring to be positioned for summer cruises along the Alaskan coastline. Repositioning cruises are not usually called that by the cruise line. It will be pretty obvious from the route. Passage on these cruises will be cheaper than the usual rates. The downside is that these routes will always be scheduled on the shoulder season of the prime vacation window.

Cruises are also a great way to vacation with grandparents or extended family. You don't have to plan complex itineraries that take into consideration everyone's interests. Each family member can choose the activities they want to participate in. Mom can go to the spa, Dad can do a shore excursion with the grandparents, and the kids can go to the pool. You can meet up again at dinner or some other pre-arranged rendezvous.

Business Plus

You have to go abroad for work. Why not take your family with you? Your employer is paying for your hotel room and your airfare, leaving you to cover the airfare for the rest of your family. Stay out of legal trouble on this one by checking your company's policy first. If the policy isn't clear, or there isn't one, make sure to get your supervisor's approval.

The downside is that it's not all fun and games. After all, you're there primarily for work reasons. Make sure your spouse and your kids know that they'll be on their own on the days when you're working. They can have an adventure and tell you all about it at dinner. Or you can add a few days at the start or the end of the trip to do things as a family. This may mean you're now covering the hotel bill on your own for that portion of the trip.

Visit friends

Sit down and make a list of all the people that you know who live overseas. Family members. Friends from high school or college. Former co-workers. A friend of a friend. Now think about where they live. There's a good chance that you know someone who lives abroad. Have they ever said, "if you're in the neighborhood, please stop by?" Now is the time to plan a visit.

Staying with friends might mean not having to pay for a hotel. This is a considerable savings in some cities. It could also mean that you have a host who knows the city and can introduce you to experiences that only locals know about.

Obviously, you will need to coordinate this type of trip in advance with your host. Don't show up unannounced. How you go about asking to stay with them will depend on how well you know them.

Definitely let them know how old your children are as well. It's polite to bring them a gift, maybe something from home that they can't get there. Depending on their work schedules and your relationship, they might give you a tour of the town or just a place to drop your luggage and sleep at night. Either way, it's more than you would have if you stayed at a hotel.

Themed Trip

Planning your trip around a theme can provide a good framework and a good start on your itinerary. If you're a runner, schedule your trip around a marathon in an exotic location. Take a trip to your ancestral homeland and trace your genealogical roots. Go on a mission trip with your church. Sign up with a volunteer organization and spend part of your vacation serving the community that you're visiting.

Pick an international event and attend it. I have a friend who travels to the summer Olympics every four years. By doing this, he's seen Sydney, Athens, Beijing and London. Another friend's family traveled to Germany to see the Passion Play in Oberammergau, an event that only happens once a decade.

The Grand Vacation

Not for the faint of heart, this can be a major expense. The word grand indicates the scale of the trip. Typical examples include touring around Europe or Southeast Asia. A grand vacation usually takes place over a summer vacation. It could last from a few weeks to a few months. However long your wallet can tolerate. I don't recommend this as the first overseas trip that you go on as a family. If you already have a few smaller trips under your belt and want to kick it up a notch, feel free to give it a go.

Round the World

Even bigger than a grand vacation, this is the classic round-the-world voyage. These can be done on any budget, depending on your comfort level and time available. Be forewarned though – to travel is to be changed. Some people set off on this trip hoping to check off a box on their bucket list and end up traveling permanently.

A quiet morning in Seoul's Bukchon Hanok village

Chapter 4
The Where - Site Selection

Site selection is more than just what country or city do you want to visit. If you have a particular destination in mind, like Machu Picchu or Paris, that's fine. Feel free to skip to the next chapter. If not, however, give some thought to the type of vacation location that you want to have based on your family's interests.

Be wary of searching for "To Do" lists on the internet. If you ask the internet for a list of attractions in the smallest town, it will likely produce a result. That doesn't mean they're actually worth visiting. A search of my hometown yields two dozen attractions, none of which I would plan an international trip around. Instead, start by thinking about your destination with questions like:

- Developed or developing country?
- English speaking or not?
- Megacity, urban, or rural?
- Beaches, mountains, or jungle?
- Peak season or off-season?
- Type of accommodations

Developed or developing?

When I was a kid, we called this "First World" and "Third World." Those terms have largely fallen out of common use. Developed countries are wealthy and industrial countries, usually with a market-based capitalist economy. Developed countries include the United States, Australia, Canada, Japan, South Korea, and most of Europe. Traveling to these countries means you'll often find well-established transit systems, potable water, and stable governments. It is also more expensive to travel in these countries.

Developing countries are going to be more of an adjustment. They may have some of the features listed above but certainly won't have all of them. Culture shock will be more intense. Health concerns will require more planning. I'm not saying don't go there. My family has had a great experience traveling in both developed and developing countries. I'm saying that thinking about it beforehand will help you to select the right destination for your family.

English speaking or not?

Traveling to a country where English is not the dominant language will definitely put you outside of your comfort zone. That's okay as long as you prepare for it. Rest assured that you will be able to find people who speak English in most major tourist destinations. You will have moments when you are lost and need to ask directions. You will have issues where things are lost in translation. You will survive.

Alternatively, you can just go to a country where English is the official language or is widely spoken. Going to a destination where English is spoken, however, does not mean that you won't have communication issues. The English language is highly adaptable and differs based on the country. This is due to accents and changes in vocabulary. Some words are used differently within the United States (cola vs. pop) so it shouldn't be a surprise that this is the case in foreign countries as well. Comparing the English spoken in Australia with the U.S. will yield differences. The differences between American English and Jamaican Patois are even greater.

Type of city

Do you want to see the sights in a big city or get away from it all in the countryside? For some, the thought of a huge metropolis can be scary. For others, it's the thought of being stuck in the middle of nowhere. This question is distinct from the question of developed world vs. developing world. There are large population centers in developing countries (Lagos, Nigeria) and there are quiet rural areas in developed countries

(Cotswolds, England). There isn't a right answer but it is worth thinking about.

Type of terrain

If you're not a fan of snow, don't go to Hokkaido, Japan in the winter. It seems obvious, but deciding what kind of terrain you want to visit can make a big difference in your family vacation. There's a high degree of variability within each terrain as well. You can summit Malaysia's highest mountain almost year-round wearing normal hiking boots with a little effort. Japan's Mount Fuji is lower in elevation but only suitable for climbing from July to early September due to weather. Other mountains require advanced training and technical expertise.

Similarly, beaches that are great for surfing are not great for snorkeling. The same beach change dramatically a few hundred feet in either direction. We visited a beach rated as one of the top ten beaches in Bali only to find it covered in trash and gritty sand with no good snorkeling or surfing conditions.

Peak season or off season?

Prices will be higher and destinations will be more crowded in peak season. But peak season varies by location. In America, we tend to think of peak season as the summer school break and the December holidays. Most schools in America have their long holiday in the summer so that makes sense. When you think internationally though, the peak season for a given destination may be different. For example, the long school break in Singapore happens in November and December.

Weather plays a role in peak seasons as well. The seasons are reversed in the southern hemisphere. That means planning a trip to New Zealand in July will put you there in the middle of winter, not summer. Some destinations, like Borneo, have a monsoon season. Sri Lanka has two monsoon seasons affecting the northeast and southwest parts of the country at different times of the year.

Festivals and holidays will affect peak season pricing as well. This includes not only big festivals like Carnival in Rio or Hong Kong's Chinese New Year but also smaller holidays like the Montreux Jazz Festival or the winter festival in Queenstown, New Zealand. Festivals can be a great experience but they will likely cost more and require more planning on your part.

Accommodations

You'll find the same range of accommodations overseas that you do in the U.S. but usually at different price points. Think about whether you want to stay in a luxury hotel with a concierge and a swimming pool, a mid-range hotel, or a budget hotel.

An all-inclusive resort may be the most economical once you factor in money saved on food, entertainment, and drinks. Be warned though, you won't see as much of the local culture if you're at a resort.

If you have older kids or a lot of kids, consider renting a house through websites like Airbnb. It will probably be cheaper than multiple hotel rooms. One of our favorite places that we've stayed was a house we rented in Bangkok on Airbnb. If you choose this option, make sure you conduct due diligence about the local laws. It's illegal to rent an apartment or house for less than six months in Singapore, but you'll still find listings on vacation rental websites.

Chapter 5
Preparation is King

It's all about the prep. Some people are free spirits who like to 'wing it.' Your first family trip abroad is not the time to do that. Free spirits of the world, relax. Having a solid plan doesn't mean that every minute of the day is planned with military precision though. It means having enough of a plan that you can react when things go wrong. To paraphrase former Defense Secretary Don Rumsfeld, there are known knowns and known unknowns. We're trying to reduce the number of known unknowns. Do that right and you'll be much better prepared to deal with the unknown unknowns.

Buy a travel book

Admittedly, this is a personal choice. Some people prefer to do their research online. I've always found that having a travel book on hand in advance makes the trip seem more real. Family members can thumb through the pages, look at pictures, get ideas and get excited about the trip. It makes a good reference when you arrive at your destination as well, with maps and phone numbers that can come in handy.

If you don't deal with guide books often, you should know that different brands cater to different audiences. While most guide books will cover the basic tourist attractions, the hotel and restaurant information will be geared towards a specific audience. Lonely Planet is geared towards budget travelers and backpackers, while Fodor's and Frommer's are aimed at those with a larger budget. Insight has lots of pictures and essays by local experts.

Passports and Visas

People show up to the airport without passports. I've seen it happen. What happens next? They aren't allowed to board the plane, that's what happens next. That's because if you manage to reach another country without a passport, you will be refused entry and sent back to your point of origin. If the country that refused entry imposes a fine, the airline will usually pass that fine on to you.

The most reliable source for information on U.S. passports is the U.S. State Department website. Processing time to get a passport is usually 4-6 weeks, so this is one of the steps that you'll have to take well in advance of your trip. You can request expedited processing, but it will cost more.

There are special requirements for passports for minors that you should be aware of as well. While adult passports are valid for ten years, passports for children younger than 16 are only valid for five years. Applications for passports for minors also have to be made in person with both parents present. This usually requires an appointment at the nearest processing center, which is often a post office.

The fee for an adult passport book is $135. The fee for a child's passport is $105. There is a cheaper option, called a passport card. The card only costs $55 for adults and $40 for children, but it is only valid for travel to Canada, Mexico, Bermuda, and the Caribbean. It is also only valid for land and sea points of entry, meaning that you can't use it to fly to another country (including Canada, Mexico, Bermuda, and the Caribbean).

A visa is permission to enter a country for a specific period of time for a specific purpose. If you are a tourist, you'll likely be given a tourist visa. When you pass through immigration at your destination, the immigration officer will stamp your passport. That stamp is the visa.

Countries determine their own policies for visas. Some countries allow you to show up and present your passport. This is known as visa on arrival. Others require you to apply for and receive a visa in advance. This is usually done through that country's embassy or consulate in your home country. Some visas take a few days to process; some take months. Some visas are free and others require a fee. The rules for each country can be found on the State Department website or the website of that country's embassy in the United States.

Many countries have enacted new policies to combat human trafficking which often targets children. Know before you go if you're going to need additional documentation to prove that your children are authorized to travel with you. Some countries will require single parents to have a letter from the other parent or court documents showing custody. In some southern African countries, you need to show original or notarized copies of children's birth certificates and occasionally your marriage certificate.

Immunizations

While you're on the State Department website researching passports, it's a good idea to check the country information for the place that you plan to visit. In addition to information about that country's visa policies, you'll find information on its currency, possible travel warnings, and recommended immunizations. Schedule appointments with your doctor to get the necessary immunizations in plenty of time. Some countries will require you to bring proof of certain immunizations, such as yellow fever.

Common travel related immunizations are listed below.

- Hepatitis A
- Hepatitis B
- Tuberculosis
- Diphtheria

- Tetanus
- Pertussis
- Measles
- Yellow Fever

Travel agents

In the age of Airbnb and Kayak, some people think travel agents are long gone. Not according to the American Society of Travel Agents, which notes that there are almost 10,000 travel agency firms operating in the U.S. Travel agents still book 85% of cruises and 50% of airline tickets. Should you use a travel agent for your trip? That depends on the type of person you are and the type of trip you're taking. Here are some factors to consider that might lead you to work with an agent instead of going it alone.

Are you booking a travel package? In addition to cruises, travel agents book 70% of all tours and travel packages. They often know about special deals and have access to pricing information that the general public does not. Package deals usually include airfare, lodging, transfers from the airport to the hotel, admission to attractions and museums, and some meals. The main advantage of a package is that most or all of the expenses are included. There are two downsides. First, you can't deviate from the package. This isn't Burger King; you don't get it your way. The second is that you're not going to venture off the beaten path. Most package tours hit the top tourist highlights in a destination and that's it.

If you're flying round-trip from Boston to Dublin and you have a hotel in mind, you probably don't need an agent to book your travel. On the other hand, if you're flying to London, taking a train to Paris and Rome, and flying home from there, you might want to consider it. I used a travel agent for a one week trip to Ireland. We drove along the southern coast from Galway to Dublin and I had specific requests for different types of lodging - 1 night in a castle, 1 night in a 5-star hotel, 2 nights at bed and breakfasts, etc. The agent handled the flights, the rental car, and all the accommodations. This is basically designing your own package tour. If you're trying to do that, a travel agent's expertise can be invaluable.

Travel agents are especially useful for specialized trips. Let's say you're not just going to France, you're doing a tour of significant battlefields from World War II. Or you're doing a kid-friendly African safari for the first time. Contacting a travel agent who specializes in the type of travel that you're interested in can save you time and money. Sure, you can try to research on your own to figure out who the best safari operators are in Botswana or how to see penguins in Antarctica. Or you can work with someone who exclusively handles that type of travel and has contacts with all the major companies in that country or region.

Some people are fine to walk out of the airport in Muscat and figure out how to flag down a taxi to a nearby hotel. Others want to have a car waiting for them; a driver holding a sign with your name on it. If you are comfortable traveling abroad, you probably don't need an agent. If you're reasonably sure that you can figure it out, you might not need an agent. But if fear of the unknown is the thing keeping you from taking the family overseas, then book a trip through an agent and go.

As it often does, this decision comes down to preference, price, and time. You can design the perfect trip all by yourself if you are willing to spend the time to research it. Or you can hire someone to do it for you.

The foods

Tasting new foods is one of the highlights of travel. Get your family excited early by going to a restaurant at home that serves food from the place that you'll be traveling to. A quick internet search should bring up all the French, Thai, or Mexican places in your area.

Try to make some of the foods at home. Recipes are easy to come by on the web. Try the website Global Table Adventure, which has recipes from every country on the planet. You can also look in cookbooks that you can get from a bookstore or library. If your grocery store doesn't have the ingredients, there's probably one nearby that does. There are grocery stores in most metropolitan areas that specialize in ingredients for Asian cooking, for example. If your city has an ethnic neighborhood (Chinatown, Little India, etc.), go for a visit one afternoon with the kids and check out the foods.

All of this will serve to make the unfamiliar less strange when you encounter it on your trip. People in general, and kids especially, like to have a sense of familiarity. It's much easier to get them to try a new food in a new setting if they've already tried something like it back home. This also gives you a chance to discuss the differences between what you encountered back home and abroad. For example, why doesn't the Chinese restaurant in Xi'an give out fortune cookies? Why does the pizza taste different in Rome than it does back home? You can also discuss what foods are "American," given that we've incorporated so many cuisines from so many places.

Cultural affairs

Want to give everyone a sneak preview of your destination? Most travel guides have suggestions for books to read before your trip for adults. Some have recommendations for kids as well. Incorporate those books into their normal reading so it doesn't seem like extra work.

As a family, watch a movie about the destination, or a TV show about the place or the local food. There are even a few shows that chronicle family travel adventures, such as Big Crazy Family Adventure on the Travel Channel. These shows give a sense of the place and usually give a sense of some of the culture shock issues that you'll encounter as well. This won't eliminate the disorientation entirely, but it will help set expectations. It will also reinforce that it is a normal reaction.

Visit an ethnic enclave in the U.S. before your trip. In sociology, an ethnic enclave is an area with a high concentration of a particular ethnicity. You're probably more familiar with the terms Little Italy, Chinatown, or Little India. Those are ethnic enclaves. If you have one of these neighborhoods nearby, take time to visit on a weekend and roam around. You'll get a small exposure to the sights, sounds, and smells that you'll encounter on your journey. Depending on the size of the neighborhood, it might be a large exposure. There's a non-comprehensive list of ethnic enclaves in North American cities on Wikipedia.

Foreign language training

English is increasingly the *lingua franca* of the world, but that doesn't mean that everyone speaks it. Sometimes you'll have a hard time understanding even those who do if they have a thick accent. And pidgin versions of English are amusing unless you're in a hurry.

The farther you roam from a tourist hot spot, the more likely it is that you'll encounter someone who doesn't speak English. We always try to learn a few key phrases in the local language and teach them to our kids. You'd be surprised how well-received it is in restaurants, hotels, and taxis. We focus on three areas for language learning:

1. Greetings: good morning, please, thank you
2. Directions: do you speak English? Where is the ____?
3. Food and numbers

A good travel guidebook will have a section in the back with basic phrases. They focus on the same three areas and often include phrases for shopping as well. Online resources are plentiful as well. Apps like Duolingo make learning a new language into a game. Duolingo has the major European languages as well as a few others and it's free. For a more comprehensive preparation, purchase a program like Rosetta Stone.

Some languages are harder for native English speakers to learn than others, but none of them are impossible. Remember, you're not aiming for college thesis level mastery; just a few icebreaker phrases.

Study a few words every night at dinner or bedtime. Use flashcards. Devise a competition with a prize for the family member who learns the most. Review the vocabulary on the flight.

Language learning is one more way to move your family outside of their comfort zone and stretch their minds. Trust me, they'll manage. They'll learn something about the culture, since culture and language are closely tied together. Some languages don't have pronouns as we understand them. Instead, people are referred to by their place in the family or society (older brother, auntie). Some languages use the same word for "he" and "she." Some languages freely adapt and borrow words from other languages (Spanish), and some societies strongly resist this (France). They'll also come home with a renewed appreciation for how hard it is for immigrants to learn English.

Packing

Most people overpack. This creates additional stress, especially if you are packing for you and for young children. Don't make the mistake of planning one outfit per day. This is a common temptation when you have young children. Some people even pack two outfits for each day, in case one gets dirty.

You'll end up with too many clothes. Multiply that by the number of family members going, and suddenly you need a few luggage carts just to get through the airport.

Pack your suitcase. Now take half of the clothes out. You'll be fine. People wear clothes at your destination. That means there are places to wash clothes. That also means you can buy more clothes if you need to.

> Notes on packing from a real traveler
> "We lay out what we think we want to wear. Then we pare down, look for overlaps, and repeat. We check one bag, for the three of us, not each. We were in Africa almost a month – one bag. Look for a place halfway through the trip where there is free or cheap laundry" - Michelle

First Aid

When traveling with kids, be sure to include a first aid kit. All prescriptions should be in original containers. Check the rules for the country you're visiting; you may need to have the signed prescriptions with you.

A basic travel first aid kit should include

- Anti-acid tablets
- Antihistamine
- Antiseptic wipes
- Band-Aids
- Sunscreen
- Aloe vera
- Hand sanitizer
- Acetaminophen and ibuprofen
- Insect repellant

Chapter 6
Expectation Management

Managing expectations is critical to the success of a family trip. While on a business trip once, I made a point to call my wife once a week. My colleague called his every night. After a few days, he asked me how I got away with only calling every seven days. Easy, I replied. We've set that expectation. If I happen to call twice in one week, I'm a hero. If you miss a day, you're a bad husband. The frequency of calls hasn't changed but the expectations are different.

Setting expectations, both yours and those of your kids, is best done early. Below are a few areas that you should give some thought to prior to the trip. Discuss them in general terms with your kids. Discuss them in detail with your spouse. And keep them in mind during the trip as well.

Squirrel: How to Deal with Shorter Attention Spans

Maybe this is the trip of a lifetime for you. Maybe you've been waiting for years to see this building in person, or to visit this city. Hopping on a flight did not radically transform your children. Whatever attention span your kids have at home is the attention span they brought with them on the trip. Keep that in mind.

When my children were younger, I was convinced that a fruit fly had a greater attention span. Growing up in the digital age, they are masters of multitasking. At least that's what their generation tells themselves. In reality, they are masters of being distracted repeatedly. This can be very frustrating when traveling if you allow it to be. We chose to capitalize on it.

When we took our kids to Paris, we wanted them to see the Louvre. It's possible to spend hours or even days in that magnificent museum, strolling through the galleries and admiring the masterpieces that stretch all the way up to the vaulted ceilings. It is not possible, however, with an eight-year-old. Set your goals a little lower and you'll find it leads to greater satisfaction for the whole family.

We made a quick list of the top 10 to 20 works of art to see in the Louvre. The big ones, so to speak. Then we blew through the museum and covered them all with a generous helping of breaks and snacks along the way. They can always go back to Paris later, or look it up online and learn more. It will be more real to them because they've seen it in person.

Expectation Management

Did our trip turn my kids into experts in the intricacies of the Renaissance movement? Not even close. But they do remember seeing the Winged Victory of Samothrace. They can identify statues of Greek gods by their accessories (winged feet, snake staff). And they don't hate museums, which can be a side effect of dragging hours on end looking at the works of Dutch masters.

> Notes from a real traveler
> "I remember taking the kids to a museum in Prague. While I was fascinated by the history, their eyes glazed over and then they started getting restless. (restless=running around like monkeys). Lesson learned!" - Kelly

One Night in Bangkok: Experiencing Nightlife

If you've taken a family vacation before, in the U.S. or abroad, this caveat should not come as a surprise. Don't expect to hit the full moon parties on the beaches of Southern Thailand with kids in tow. Much like when you are home, your ability to enjoy the nightlife while traveling will depend to a large extent on the age of your children, your comfort level with leaving them in the care of sitters, and your desire to party like you're twenty-five again.

Keep the local culture in mind as well. If your kids are young, you're probably looking to hit a restaurant and be back at the hotel before 7 p.m. If you're in Spain, however, you may find that the restaurants don't open for dinner before 7 p.m. So what do you do? As always, you live like the locals. Settle in for a nap in the afternoon and take the kids to dinner later.

Sometimes you want an evening without kids. On a short trip of a week or less, you may not feel this urge. The longer the trip, the more it will seem like a good idea. If you're staying at a decent hotel (i.e. an expensive one,) the concierge should be able to provide a list of babysitters or arrange for one for you. If not, try searching the local expat websites for suggestions.

Food Fights: It's Okay to Eat McDonald's

We don't eat much fast food as a family. That changed when we went to Japan. My son was four years old at the time. We ate at McDonald's every third day, just to make sure that he actually ate because he was not a fan of trying new foods. Then we left Tokyo. On our way to a remote ryokan near Mount Fuji, I tried to prepare him for the tragedy that was to come.

"Listen," I explained. "There won't be a McDonald's near the new hotel. So you have to eat whatever we order, ok?"

He nodded his little head soberly. He had the last laugh, though. After two trains and a bus, we pulled up to a rural bus station. Perched in the corner window of the building were the familiar golden arches. "See, dad," he said smiling. "There's nothing to worry about."

Food is an area where I am willing to compromise with my kids, up to a point. Put yourself in their shoes. They've been pulled away from everything they know as familiar. There are strange sounds, strange smells, and signs in languages that they can't read. Suddenly, they see a familiar trademark sign above an

American franchise. Indulge them. Up to a point, that is. After all, travel is partly about getting out of your comfort zone. My suggestion is to take a two-pronged approach.

The first prong is to agree in advance when you will, collectively as a family, try new foods. Doing this in advance is very important. Springing congee on a kid at 7:00 a.m. when he has his heart set on waffles (for the third day in a row) is a recipe for disaster. If it's breakfast, discuss it the night before. If it's dinner, mention it in the afternoon.

The second prong is to give in. Order the fast food from time to time. But while you're giving in, make it a learning experience. Talk about how the food is different than it is in America. I don't just mean ordering a Royale with Cheese instead of a Quarterpounder. Spend some time looking at the menu in the restaurant. Ask your kids how the menu is different from the one that they're used to. All of the McDonald's restaurants in Malaysia, for example, are certified halal. Ask them why that might be.

You never know what will stick either. One of my kids loves sushi from our time in Japan eight years ago. He liked chopsticks so much that he eats his cereal with them. Now he's the most adept chopstick-er in the whole family.

Playgrounds and Beaches: Adding Kid Stuff

It can't all be museums. Going to a playground or park can be a great way to let kids run off some energy. They might meet local kids and learn a new game or two. Get your kids involved by letting them pick some of the attractions that you'll visit. They're likely to pick the beach or the zoo. Maybe even a movie.

Much like the fast food, going to the movie theater in another country can be an educational experience as well. How do the ticket prices compare to the prices back home? What about the commercials they show before the movie? Do they have subtitles? We've noticed that movies are even edited for content when shown in more conservative countries.

Chapter 7
And We're Off!

Now you've done it. All that preparation has paid off and you're boarding the train or plane for your adventure. Humorist Robert Benchley famously said, "In America there are two classes of travel - first class, and with children." Pithy saying, but there's also the old adage that getting there is half the fun.

> **Travel Tip:** Don't leave home without making sure that you have:
>
> - Passports and visas
> - Plane tickets
> - Cash and credit cards
> - Snacks for the trip
> - Leave your travel plans, contact info, and photocopies of passports with a friend or relative

There's a little truth to both. We're going to be optimists though and lean towards the latter. Here are a few things to keep in mind so that you'll still have your sanity when you arrive at your destination.

These tips are geared towards air travel but can apply to other forms of transportation as well. I'm also writing mostly for those with economy class tickets. If you're traveling with kids and you've opted for business or first class, you can expect even more in terms of choices.

Toys for the plane / train

If you've flown with your kids domestically, the main difference with traveling internationally is the duration of the flights. It's only four and a half hours by plane from Chicago to Los Angeles. It takes almost twice that long to get from Chicago to Frankfurt, Germany. And you could almost fly round-trip from Chicago to Los Angeles twice in the time it takes to go non-stop from Dallas to Sydney, Australia. That's a lot of time in the air with kids who probably don't want to sit for that long.

After years of travel, my kids are very comfortable on planes, trains, ferries, and even rickshaws. They do better on an eight-hour flight than a 20-minute ride across town. A five-hour flight feels short to us, probably because it takes almost 24 hours of travel to get back to the United States right now. If this is your first trip, however, that may not be the case.

These days, planes have pretty sophisticated in-flight entertainment options. The longer the flight, the more choices you're going to have. If you have strong feelings about TV and movie ratings, you can even ask about setting parental controls on your child's screen to limit what he's watching.

When we first started traveling with our kids, portable electronic devices were not common. We packed old lunchboxes with crayons, coloring books and small toys like cars and action figures. As they grew older, we added books and tablets loaded with games and videos.

I still recommend packing a kit like this. For tweens and older, make them responsible for selecting their own materials. This gives them a sense of ownership and makes them feel like they're contributing to the trip.

With all those options, the hardest part may be peeling your kids away from their screens. Manage expectations early by setting limits on how many shows they can watch. Get them to sleep and get some sleep yourself. The cabin crew dims the lights on long flights, which helps.

In-flight Meals

I remember taking a ten-hour non-stop flight from Honolulu to Newark. A few hours into the flight, I asked when the meal service would happen. I was so used to flying overseas that I had forgotten domestic flights don't include meals.

Check the airline website to see if they offer a child's meal option. Two of the three major U.S. airlines (Delta and United) have special meals for children on international flights. Many foreign airlines do as well. You'll need to order it in advance, usually at least 24 hours prior to the flight.

Immigration and Passport Control

If you've never gone through immigration and customs with kids, it can be a little overwhelming. There are signs everywhere. No talking! No pictures! No cell phone use! Stay behind the line until you are called! Relax. Most immigration officials are going to be patient with you if you have small children. They will usually let you and a child (or two if need be) go through together.

This can be a very confusing time for kids. They're tired from the long flight. They're suffering from jet lag. All of the signs are probably in a different language (but probably also in English). There could be strange sights or smells. They look to you for reassurance. Except guess what? All of those things apply to you as well.

Rest assured, you will get through this and have a great trip. But first you have to get through immigration and customs. I recommend talking through this process with your children before you deplane. Explain that it may be confusing and hectic. Explain that you have to be quiet and patient and wait in line at immigration to be allowed into the country. Explaining this sets their expectations so they don't think you'll walk off the plane and right into a waiting taxi. It could take 30-60 minutes to get through immigration, get your luggage, and clear customs. Letting kids know that in advance can help forestall a potential meltdown.

Losing your passport is going to put a huge damper on your trip. This is a very valuable document, so you will be tempted not to trust it to your child. I agree. Now that I have tweens and teenagers, I pass out passports just prior to immigration checkpoints and have them go through the checkpoint alone. If there are two adults, send one through before the first child. That way there's an adult on the other side to wait with the kids in case one of you gets held up for some reason. After we clear immigration, I collect the passports and keep them for the rest of the trip.

Conquering Jet Lag

Jet lag hits children harder than adults. Traveling east tends to create worse jet lag than traveling west. A general planning factor is that it will take one day per time zone crossed to fully adjust. Traveling by train or boat makes this easier because you're traveling slower. Knowing that and planning for it can help. Short trips by plane, however, mean that you could be battling jet lag for the duration of the trip. Here are some recommendations to help beat it.

- Drink lots of water.
- Adjust your watches to the new time zone as soon as you take off.
- Eat and sleep as much as possible on the new schedule while flying.
- Stay up when you land until nighttime (assuming your children no longer nap). Naps will just delay your adjustment.
- Get outside. Sunshine and fresh air will help energize you.

Travel with Kids

The folks back home - keeping in touch

Sometimes people back home didn't think it was a good idea for you to travel. They may have even told you this. Like the time my wife flew from New York to Doha with two kids under the age of seven. Relieve some of their concerns by dropping a quick text or email to let them know you arrived. This usually means grandparents and friends.

Beware of data roaming charges on your phone, or you could end up with a very large bill when you get home. I've found it easy and cheap to get a phone card in every country I've ever been to (except the United States). Get one at the airport or a convenience store. Otherwise, wait to use the wi-fi at the hotel.

Capable Kids: Children are more capable than we usually give them credit for. Don't do all the work yourself. Below are tips for how to get them to help based on age. You know your children best; adjust accordingly.

4-6 year olds can
- carry/pull their own carry-on
- use the in-flight entertainment system

7-10 year olds can
- pack their own carry-on

11-13 year olds can
- go through immigration checkpoint solo
- figure out bus/train timetables

Children ages 14 and older can
- go get snacks
- watch younger siblings
- do whatever you need done

Travel with Kids

A bustling market street in Germany

Chapter 8
Culture Shock

What is culture shock?

Culture shock is the disorientation you feel when you first experience a new country or place. It is caused by the disconnect between what you expect and what you experience when encountering another culture.

We all bring pre-conceived notions into situations. These pre-conceived notions serve as mental shortcuts to help us navigate social interactions and other experiences. When dealing with another culture, these shortcuts don't work.

It can be as simple as having to look right instead of left before crossing the street because the country has left hand traffic. It can be more complex, like signs and menus in an alphabet that you can't read. Your brain stares at the sign, expecting it to make sense but it doesn't. Something that you subconsciously think should be automatic suddenly isn't. Then frustration sets in.

Coping with culture shock – Before the trip

Are you excited about the trip? Talk about it with your kids. They can tell if you're dreading it. If you approach this adventure with the same enthusiasm that you have for a root canal, they will sense it. If that's your perspective, it's better not to go. On the other hand, if you're excited, talk about it.

When do you talk about it? Anytime. In the car. At dinner. Shopping for clothes. The key is to weave it into the conversation with open-ended questions. If you're at dinner, ask, "What do you think we'll eat when we go to . . .?"

Ask what they're looking forward to about the trip. Ask what they are concerned about. Find out the answers to their questions. Even better, help them to find the answers themselves.

Coping with culture shock – During the trip

No matter how much you prepare, culture shock is going to happen. The important thing to realize and to share with your kids is that this is normal. With older kids and teenagers, this can start with a discussion of culture shock like the ones at the beginning of this chapter. With younger kids, you'll have to simplify it a lot.

The gut reaction of a lot of people when they encounter these difficulties is, "why can't they just do it like we do it at home?" If this comes up, it's good to remind your family that you are the visitors in the foreign country. They do things this way because it works for them. It's not that one way or the other is correct – they're just different.

Culture shock affects everyone differently. On a short trip, it may be possible to tolerate it until you get home. Children are more susceptible to it because they are more emotional and because they have less control over the situation than their parents. Maybe you notice that family members are apathetic (in the case of teenagers, more apathetic than usual). Other signs might include trouble sleeping, loss of appetite or irritability.

Simply being aware of culture shock does a great deal to help cope with it. A sense of the familiar helps, so you may find that children are comforted by a blanket or stuffed animal at an age when they normally would not rely on them anymore. When you sense a crisis building, reset everyone's attitude with an unexpected treat, like ice cream or a souvenir.

The peaceful quiet of the ruins at Angkor Wat

Chapter 9
Surviving Re-entry

Culture shock is the disorientation you feel when you first experience a new country or place. Similarly, re-entry refers to the period of adjustment that you will experience when you come home. If you were only gone for a weekend, re-entry probably won't take much. There will be some jet lag, but your kids will bounce back pretty quickly.

If you're gone longer, re-entry might be more involved. The longer you've been traveling or the more exotic the location, the more they will have changed. They've had new experiences and seen new things. Their worldview has expanded. That's ok – that was part of the point of traveling, right? You should expect a period of adjustment as they move back into their old routines. Disorientation is common. Here are some ways to reinforce what they learned and to help them to re-adjust to home.

Get back to routine

Routines are important. Your routine was disrupted while you were traveling. Chores weren't done, bedtimes were adjusted, homework didn't happen. Now that you're back home, it's time to start all of those routines again.

I'm warning you, there will be resistance. After all, who wants to go back to chores and homework? This is normal and will subside with a little patience on your part and a little effort on theirs. It helps to set the tone by getting back to your own routines. This will probably happen naturally since you have to go back to work.

Talk about your trip

So what do you do with all the experiences that you had? Talk about them. Discussing it helps to reinforce their memories of the trip. It helps them to make connections from their daily lives to the lives of people that they met on the trip.

You have to be a little sneaky here. Kids won't respond well to this if it seems formalized. Instead, suggest connections when they occur naturally. Eating dinner with chopsticks might remind everyone of the trip to Tokyo. Seeing an article in the paper might remind you of Spain. Their schoolwork probably includes a session on geography or social studies that will tie in with your trip. When that happens, don't say, "Remember when . . . ?" That leads to a yes or no answer. Instead, ask, "What do you remember about when we were in . . . ?"

Younger children can bring something to Show and Tell at school like a souvenir that they bought. Older children may choose to write about their experience in an essay for school or an article for the school newspaper.

Be ready for random connections

Kids make connections in their brains that adults sometimes don't. When that happens, ask them to explain. Watching Ferris Bueller's Day Off recently, my son noticed the painting that Cameron stares at in the Art Institute of Chicago. The painting is *A Sunday Afternoon on the Island of La Grande Jatte* by George Seurat. It's a good example of pointillism, a technique that developed from Impressionism. My son exclaimed, "We saw that painting in Paris!"

We haven't seen that painting because we haven't been to the Art Institute of Chicago. We have, on the other hand, been to the Museum d'Orsay in Paris, which houses impressionist works by artists like Monet, Manet, and Degas. This connection that he made allowed us to discuss a whole range of topics, like how artists draw inspiration from one another and why some art is in one museum versus another museum.

This conversation only happened because we didn't default to saying, "no, you're wrong. We've never seen that painting." Instead we asked, "Why do you say that?" and the conversation got rolling from there.

Temper their expectations about re-entry

It's often said that the only thing worse that looking at your old vacation photos is looking at someone else's. Not everyone wants to hear about your awesome, life-changing travel experience. You probably realize that. Your kids may not. This is another teachable moment. You can help them to not become insufferable travel snobs. Yes, they've had a tremendous privilege in being able to travel. Not everyone has that, and not everyone wants that. Every sentence shouldn't start with, "well, when I was in Argentina this summer."

Chapter 10
Travel with Infants

I think anxiety about international travel with infants is the leading cause of the belief that travel with children is impossible. This is especially true if it's your first child. You've read multiple books on child-rearing and your anxiety level is high.

You don't want to expose your child to exotic diseases. Or you're exhausted just getting through daily life and you can't imagine trying to do this on vacation in a foreign country.

Advantages of travel with infants

There are advantages to traveling with infants though. For one thing, they don't complain about the destination. They don't get a vote. Also, you can hold infants under the age of two on flights rather than pay for an extra seat. Take advantage of that while you can.

Infants are content to eat and sleep wherever you go. They will sleep in their stroller as you take your time in the art gallery or stop for a coffee at a bistro. Infants need food, clean diapers, and lots of snuggling. You can do this anywhere on the planet. Plus that stroller comes in handy for storage.

Another advantage is that they are easily amused. The same toys that pacify them at home will work on the road. Kids in general are great for connecting with locals when you travel. Babies are especially good for this.

Most of the advantages that apply to infants also apply to toddlers. Even when they get upset, they are easy to redirect. A quick snack or small souvenir can work wonders. They're not in school yet, which means you can travel during off-peak periods and save money.

Disadvantages of travel with infants

There are several disadvantages to travel with infants. They can't tell you when they're too hot, too cold, or not feeling good. The fact that they can't talk means you have to be extra vigilant about hydration and insulation.

When it comes to moving from one place to another, they are not contributing members of the family. Infants are net detractors from mobility. Not only do they not contribute by carrying their own suitcase, they frequently are the cause of the excess baggage that you'll end up checking.

Toddlers

Toddlers are worse than infants because they are mobile. That means you have to keep track of them and all the other stuff. I can carry everything I need for a month of travel in a backpack but I've also filled a minivan just to take young kids to the beach.

Infants and toddlers will limit the kinds of trips you can take. Obviously, you're not going to take them on high adventure trips like scuba diving or rock climbing.

Recommendations

How do you travel with infants and toddlers? Enjoy the fact that they are easily amused and don't have much of a say in your itinerary. Plan trips to places you want to go and do things that you want to do. Enjoy the extra storage that comes from having a stroller. Travel in the off-season and enjoy the smaller crowds and the cheaper prices.

Below are some other recommendations

- Select destinations that are stroller friendly
- Ask your doctor about necessary immunizations and safety precautions
- If you are particular about brands for diapers, soap, etc., be sure to bring sufficient supplies with you
- When making flight reservations, ask about a bassinet. Most airlines can attach one to the bulkhead after take-off
- Consider whether you need to bring a car seat

- Ask the hotel concierge about arranging for a babysitter so you can spend a night alone.

Chapter 11
Travel with Teenagers

Teenagers have a reputation for being moody, self-absorbed, and difficult. That reputation is well-deserved. They also are almost adults. That means if you haven't exposed them to travel yet, you don't have much time left to do so.

Teenagers are old enough to start understanding the world around them. They will absorb new surroundings and ask questions. They can also understand the answers. If your teen studies a foreign language, traveling to a country that speaks that language can be a great opportunity to reinforce the usefulness of that skill.

Advantages of travel with teenagers

Most of the disadvantages of travel with infants are advantages now. They can carry their own weight, both literally and figuratively. They can be responsible for their own suitcase, their own belongings. They can be left alone for a few hours. They can tell you when they don't feel good and why.

They can be part of the trip in a way that younger kids cannot. Trips focused on more adventurous activities, such as scuba diving or trekking, become more feasible with teenagers.

Disadvantages of travel with teenagers

Teenagers want to be independent of their parents. Developmentally, this is normal and a positive thing. They have a tendency, however, to express that desire in whiny and negative ways. They can rebel by not listening or doing what they're told. At home, this is upsetting. In some countries or situations, this is life-threatening.

Teenagers don't want to spend every minute of the vacation with their parents. They may not even want to go on vacation. They may not understand the way relationships work in the country you're visiting, which can lead to embarrassing misunderstandings.

Recommendations

Traveling with teens involves the same type of balance that living with teens does – balance between looking out for them and teaching them to look out for themselves.

Enforced small spaces can remove some of the barriers to communication that exist at home by forcing you to spend more time together. You're in a small hotel room or suite instead of a large house. Use that time to your advantage. Explain how much you appreciate their help with things like luggage and younger siblings. If you are lost or confused, admit it. They will appreciate your honesty.

Below are some other recommendations

- Anticipate potential friction points before leaving home
- Set clear expectations for activities that the family will do together
- Work with your teenager to plan separate activities she can do alone or with a group
- Create ground rules for screen time
- Give teens responsibility for their own passports, luggage, etc.
- Consider an all-inclusive resort or high adventure activity
- If you get phone cards, get one for your teen as well
- Consider letting him bring a close friend along on the trip

A tasty Thai dish

Chapter 12
Lifelong travel

You've successfully applied the tips in this book to take a family trip overseas. It was a triumph. You had a great time.

It ignites a passion in your heart for travel, a passion that your partner and your kids share. You eagerly plan your next trip. Years down the road, you realize that you've raised kids who love to experience new places and new cultures. Here are some ways to keep that going.

Study abroad

Many schools offer the chance for high school students or college students to spend a semester studying abroad. High school students will live with a host family.

For high school students, the best time to do this is sophomore or junior year. This ensures that you have time to complete graduation requirements and college applications when you return.

Some of these programs come with scholarship funding, while others have to be financed by the individual. It's important to do your research and make sure that you're working with a reputable organization that clearly spells out all the costs of the program in advance. For high school students, consult with your guidance counselor. For college students, talk to the registrar or international programs office at your school.

Study abroad programs include:
- Congress-Bundestag Youth Exchange
- German-American Partnership Program
- Kennedy-Lugar Youth Exchange & Study (YES) Abroad
- National Security Language Initiative for Youth

Host an exchange student

Open your home to an exchange student from another country. You and your kids will make a lifelong friend and get to learn about another culture. This can also open the door to reciprocal hosting in his home country.

Penpal

When I was a kid, penpal had a very literal meaning. You wrote letters to someone in another country and that person wrote you back.

With today's technology, penpal can be much more interactive. You can use social media and online chat programs to keep in touch with someone that you met during your travels or practice a foreign language with a native speaker.

"Gap Year"
Gap years have been common in the United Kingdom for many years. They are increasingly popular in the United States. Students graduate from high school and travel for a year before entering college. Colleges have started to recognize this as a valuable experience and sometimes will grant deferrments for students who have already been accepted so that they can have a gap year. Students tend to mature quite a bit in that year and therefore enter college better prepared to focus and study.

There are many ways to do this and several good books on the subject (see Travel Resources, chapter 13). There are even travel agents who specialize in booking gap year airfare with multiple city stops. For students planning to take a gap year, it's not necessary to map out the whole year in advance. That would defeat the point of learning by experience. It is useful, however, to develop a rough budget and a rough timeline.

Traveling as a Career
There are lots of jobs that involve travel. If your child has caught the travel bug, she may want to look into a career as a:

Diplomat/State Department – The U.S. State Department is the oldest department in the Executive branch.

The State Department represents the interests of the United States at more than 270 locations around the world, including embassies, consulates, and missions to international organizations. The Department offers opportunities to work as Foreign Service Officers (Generalists), Foreign Service Specialists and Civil Service professionals.

Peace Corps Volunteer – This is not a career but it's a great way to spend a few years helping others. The Peace Corps was founded in 1961 to promote world peace and friendship. Volunteers typically spend two years working in a community overseas to help train people in education, agriculture, or a host of other projects. More than 200,000 Americans have volunteered with the Peace Corps since it was created.

Military – The U.S. military has troops stationed in over 150 countries, with the largest concentrations in Germany, Italy, Japan and Korea. An enlistment tour has a specified length, usually 3-5 years. Benefits can include college tuition assistance. A recruiter will be glad to talk to you about options but it's best to do some research first and have an idea what you want before you walk into his office.

Travel writer – Travel the world, write about it, and get paid for it. Sounds like a dream come true, right? Of course, there's more to it than that. There are travel writers who edit the travel guides and then there are travel writers who do long form articles and books (Bill Bryson, Paul Theroux). If you are interested in this kind of job, start by reading those who are doing it already and working on several freelance pieces.

Events planner – The job title aptly describes the position. Events planners help to plan and execute events. These can be small events like weddings or large and specialized events like trade shows or concerts.

Journalist – Similar to travel writing, I recommend starting with a strong background in English and working on a local or school newspaper.

Tour Guide – Tour guides help other people to travel. There are many ways to specialize in this field; by location, by type of travel, by size of group. You could be a divemaster taking people to Palau or a leading a historical tour of Israel. Successful tour guides have several things in common though. They like meeting new people, they have strong communication and problem solving skills, and they are comfortable working independently.

Flight attendant – There are several tell-all books and articles about life as a flight attendant. Check one out and see if this is something you are still interested in. Every airline has its own rules for assigning routes and seniority plays a big part. This is a job that is defined by traveling.

Digital nomad – Globalization and the digital economy have made it easy to set up and run a business remotely, giving rise to the subculture of digital nomads. There are piano teachers, accountants, copywriters, and graphic designers working in this space. You have to have strong computer skills and a skill that people are willing to pay for.

A fair warning in Bali

Chapter 13
Travel Resources

Books about travel

The Practical Nomad by Edward Hasbrouck
ISBN:978-1-59880-888-9; 712 pages, Avalon Travel.
A one-stop resource for planning a round-the-world voyage.

The Passport by Martin Llody
ISBN: 0-7509-2964-2; 2003, 282 pages, Sutton Publishing
A fascinating look at the history of individual travel documents (passports) throughout history.

Raising Global Nomads by Robin Pascoe
ISBN: 0-9686760-3-0; 2006, 229 pages, Expatriate Press.
Robin's book deals honestly and openly with the challenges and joys of raising children internationally.

Wide-Open World by John Marshall
ISBN: 978-0-345-54964-8; 2015, 329 pages, Ballantine.
A riveting tale of one family's life-changing year volunteering as they travel around the world.

Travel with Children
ISBN: 978-1-740-59502-5; 2009, 288 pages, Lonely Planet
In addition to useful tips and tricks, this book offers suggestions on places to go with kids in various locations around the globe. The categories are largely broken down by continent.

500 Places to Take Your Kids Before They Grow Up by Holly Hughes
ISBN: 978-0-7645-9588-2; 2006, 567 pages, Frommer's.
This book's target audience is the U.S., so there is a heavy emphasis on U.S. destinations. For example, Wall Drug in South Dakota gets as much coverage as the entire country of Thailand. It is a great starting point to get ideas for travel though, and there is a newer edition that was published in 2009.

The Art of Travel by Alain de Botton
ISBN: 0-375-72534-2; 2002, 255 pages, Vintage Books.
This is less a guide to destinations and more a philosophical treatise on travel and how it changes us. It is densely packed and masterfully written.

1,000 Places to See Before You Die by Patricia Schultz
ISBN: 978-0-7611-0484-1; 2003, 974 pages, Workman.
A great book to curl up on the couch and daydream with. Let those daydreams turn into travel itineraries! There is a U.S. focus (the U.S. takes up almost 200 pages) but it is a good starting point to identify what to do when you get to a place.

Off the Tourist Trail
ISBN: 978-0-7566-5399-6; 2009, 336 pages, DK Pub.
Just the foreword by Bill Bryson makes this book worth getting. Full of terrific pictures, this book proposes alternatives to the heavily worn tourist sites around the world. Instead of Machu Picchu, for example, try Bolivia's Isla del Sol.

The Complete Guide to the Gap Year
ISBN: 978-0-4704-2526-8; 2009, 264 pages, Jossey-Bass.
This is the self-described "go-to" book for planning a gap year.

Travel Guides

There are dozens of companies that produce travel guides these days. The five below (listed alphabetically) will cover the needs of most travelers.

- Fodor's
- Frommers
- Insight
- Lonely Planet
- Rough Guides

Internet

Any list of internet resources is prone to obsolescence faster than a list of printed resources. Despite that, below that are some sites that I've found useful in planning travel for my family. I hope they are useful for your family.

Airbnb – www.airbnb.com. This isn't the first vacation rental website, but it is the fastest growing and most well-known.

Bootsnall - www.bootsnall.com. BootsnAll specializes in independent travel. They have a 30-day course on how to plan a round-the-world trip for a family.

City Pass – Each city pass website is unique. It's best to do an internet search based on the city (London Pass, Barcelona Pass, etc.)

Eurail - www.eurail.com. The Eurail pass has several options based on the number of countries you plan to visit and how many days you plan to travel.

Extra Pack of Peanuts - extrapackofpeanuts.com. Travis Sherry's website and podcast are a great resource for travel. He has a guide to using hotel points and frequent flier miles as well as destination guides.

Hostels.com – www.hostels.com. This website lists more hostels worldwide than any other site.

ITA Matrix – matrix.itasoftware.com. ITA Matrix is a search engine for checking airline ticket prices. It is the backbone of sites like Kayak and Hipmunk.

Nomadic Dragon – www.nomadicdragon.com. My blog has stories about travel, tips, and interviews with other ordinary people who've chosen a life filled with travel.

Price of Travel - www.priceoftravel.com. Want to know how much a taxi should cost from the airport to the city center in Siem Reap, Cambodia? Or how much you'll pay for a mid-range hotel in Santiago, Chile? Price of Travel has those numbers for you.

Seat 61 – www.seat61.com. Started as a hobby by a rail enthusiast, this site gives you all the information you need to travel by train anywhere in the world.

Skyscanner – www.skyscanner.com. Skyscanner allows you to search for cheap airline tickets. One feature that I really like is that you can search by country "Germany" or type in "anywhere" and find the cheapest flights on given dates.

Travelfish – www.travelfish.org. Travelfish covers travel in Southeast Asia. Their writers visit every site that they write about, and they always pay their own way. This gives them legitimacy in my book.

Travel with Kids

Trekaroo - www.trekaroo.com. Trekaroo helps families travel, especially in the U.S. and Canada. It's a great resource for getting started.

Acknowledgements

First and foremost, I would like to thank my wife. She is the first person to read my drafts and the biggest supporter of my hobby. I also need to thank my children. Writing a book while working a full-time job inevitably means spending less time with your family. This being my third book, that goes threefold.

Special thanks goes to those who have contributed their own thoughts about traveling with kids to improve this work, including Kelly, Michelle, Nichole, and Stacy.

Index

advantages of travel, 2-4
Airbnb, 31, 37, 84
airfare
    discount, 10
    infant fares, 67
    using points/miles, 10
    websites, 10
attention span, 46-47
attractions, saving money on, 12
babysitters, 48, 70
Barcelona, 1, 12
Berlin, 1, 12
Big Crazy Family Adventure, 40
Borneo, 31
Budgeting, 9-18
debt, 12
Caribbean, 13, 21, 22, 35
child meals, 53
Chinatown, 39, 40
City pass, 14, 15, 17, 18, 84
Colombo, 12
Concierge, 31, 48, 70
Congress-Bundestag Youth Exchange, 76
connecting rooms, 10, 14, 15, 18

Index

cruises, 13, 19, 21-22, 37
culture shock, 28, 40, 59-61, 63
Customs and Immigration, 35-36, 54-55, 57
developed countries, 28-29
developing countries, 9, 28-30
Dublin, 1, 12, 37-38
Duolingo, 41
ethnic enclaves, 40-41
Eurail, 10, 84
Europe, 1, 10, 11, 12, 20-21, 24, 28, 41
exchange students, 76
expectation management, 45-50
Extra Pack of Peanuts, 11, 84
first aid kit, 43-44
Fodor's, 34, 83
food, 10, 11, 14-18, 31, 39-41, 48-50, 68
foreign language training, 41-42
frequent flier miles, 10, 84
Frommer's, 34, 82, 83
Gallup poll, 5
gap year, 77, 83
German-American Partnership Program, 76
Hotels
    Concierge, 31, 48, 70
    connecting rooms, 10, 14, 15, 18
    foreign brands, 11
    luxury, 6, 31
    U.S. brands, 11

       using points to book, 11
Hong Kong, 12, 31
Immunizations, 7, 36-37, 69
immigration, 35-36, 54-55, 57
infants
       tips for traveling with, 67-70
In-flight entertainment, 52, 57
Insight, 34, 83
ITA Matrix, 10, 85
Japan, 2, 10, 28, 30, 48-49, 78
jet lag, 20, 54, 55, 63
Kayak, 37, 85
Kennedy-Lugar Youth Exchange & Study (YES)
      Abroad, 76
kids meals, 53
Kuala Lumur, 9
Kyoto, 2
language training, 41-42
Little India, 39-40
Little Italy, 40
London, 6, 12, 18, 24, 38, 84
Lonely Planet, 34, 82, 83
Louvre, 46
luxury hotel, 6, 31
monsoon season, 31
Munich, 1
National Security Language Initiative for Youth, 76
non-peak season, 9, 10, 20, 22, 28, 30-31, 69

Index

Paris, 6, 12, 20, 27, 38, 46, 65
Penpal, 76-77
off-season, 9, 10, 20, 22, 28, 30-31, 69
package tours, 37-38
passports, 5, 7, 12, 34-36, 51, 54-55, 73, 81
    how to apply for, 34-36
    passport control, 35-36, 54-55, 57
peak season, 28, 30-31
Peace Corps, 78
Prague, 47
private jet, 6
rail passes, 10
re-entry, 63-66
repositioning cruise, 22
Rome, 1, 7, 17, 38, 40
Rough Guides, 83
ryokan, 2, 48
sample budgets
    Atlanta to Rome, 17
    Chicago to Montreal, 14
    Houston to Antigua, 16
    Los Angeles to Seoul, 15
    Miami to Caribbean, 13
    New York to London, 18
Sherry, Travis, 11, 84
Singapore, 9, 12, 30, 32
site selection, 27-32
Skyscanner, 10, 85

strollers, 2, 68, 69
study abroad programs, 76
Taipei, 12
teenagers
    tips for traveling with, 71-74
Tokyo, 2, 12, 48, 64
travel agents, 37-39, 77
Travel Channel, 40
traveling with debt, 12
trip selection
    business trip, 22-23
    cruise, 21-22
    Grand vacation, 24
    Round-the-world, 25
    themed vacation, 24
    visit friends, 23-24
    weekender, 20-21
United Kingdom, 5, 77
Vienna, 12
Visas, 7, 34-36, 51
weekend trips, 14, 18, 20-21

Edward Cox is an author and travel writer. From 2008 to 2011, he was an assistant professor of American Politics, Public Policy and Strategy in the Department of Social Sciences at the U.S. Military Academy, West Point, NY.

Ed graduated from the United States Military Academy in 1998 with a bachelor's degree in political science and a commission as a lieutenant of armor. He graduated from the Maxwell School at Syracuse University in 2008 with master's degrees in public administration and international relations.

Ed is an Eagle Scout and enjoys camping, hiking, writing and traveling. His other books include *Grey Eminence: Fox Conner and the Art of Mentorship* and *Camping on Oahu*.

The most famous general that you've never heard of.

Fox Conner graduated from West Point in 1898 and fought in the Spanish-American War. He served as General Pershing's lead planner in World War I. During the interwar period, he trained Eisenhower, Marshall, and Patton to fight World War II. Each of them described him as the smartest boss that they ever had.

Grey Eminence is the first biography of this pivotal military leader.

"Edward Cox has written a fascinating portrait of one of our nation's great soldiers."– Brian D. Shaw, President, The George C. Marshall Foundation

"Ed Cox's book serves as a premier case study" – Don Vandergriff, author of *Raising the Bar: Creating and Nurturing Adaptability to Deal with the Changing Face of War*

Camping in Paradise

Hawaii is America's paradise.

Camping on Oahu provides the only comprehensive guide to Oahu's state, county, and private campgrounds.

Includes:
- how to book
- facilities
- recommendations
- campground maps
- camping tips
- Hawaiian language

The game about living overseas

- Expats
- Diplomats
- Military
- Third Culture Kids
- Gamers

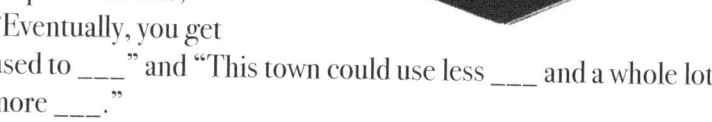

The Expat Life game is a phrase-matching game. Players take turns picking the best answers to questions like, "Eventually, you get used to ___" and "This town could use less ___ and a whole lot more ___."

The Expat Life game features easy rules and quick set up so you don't waste time. It's a compact card game, so you can throw it in your bag and bring it to a friend's house. The endless combinations of questions and answers will have you laughing right away. The familiar scenarios will have you swapping stories

Available at www.ExpatLifeGame.com and through Amazon.com.

Made in the USA
San Bernardino, CA
28 August 2017